You're Never Too Big To Hold

by Barbara Bassett

To Order This Book
(Online or by Phone)

www.nevertoobigtohold.com
573-443-4343

Pre-press production by Studio 1011, Sandy Hockenbury, Designs for print, web and mobile media

Published and distributed by Roundabout Press, Columbia, MO
Email: roundaboutpress@gmail.com

Library of Congress 2010911947
ISBN 978-0-615-39723-8
Printed in the USA by Walsworth Print Group, Marceline, MO

To Danielle, Deborah and Tracy
— who held me
when I needed it most —

And to everyone else
who has held me since

Whenever you're feeling sort of sick, and have to stay in bed...

Whenever
you're sad
and lonely,
and the world
seems dark
and cold...

It doesn't matter
how big you are,
you're never
too big to hold.

If you're tall, you can easily fold,

So you're never too big to hold.

You don't have to lose a pound,

'Cause you're never too big to hold.

No, you're never too big to hold,
no matter what you've been told!

For even if you're so incredibly strong...

You're still never too big to hold.

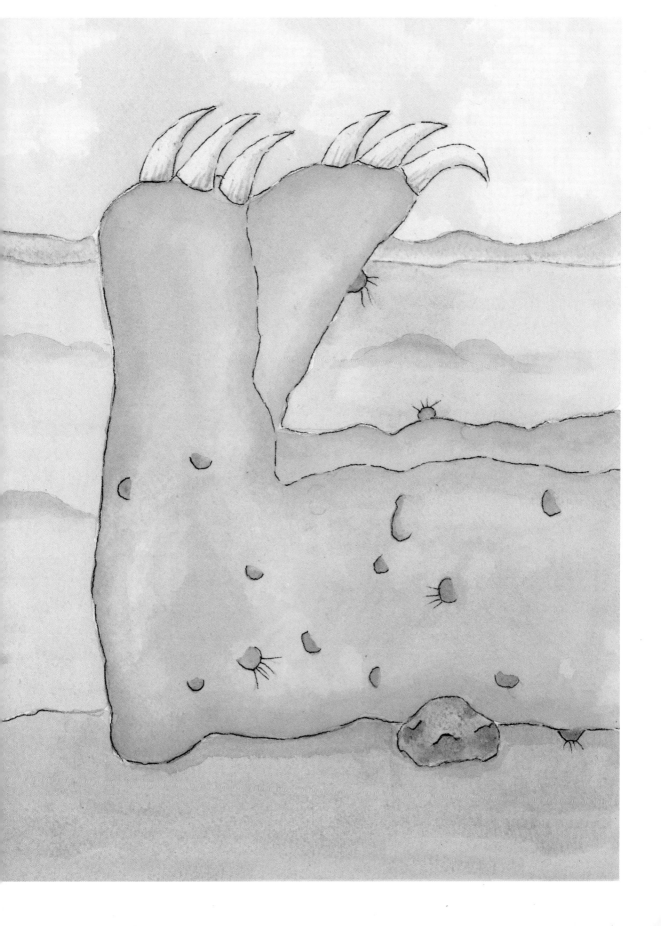

You're just never too big to hold! Not even when you're old!

You may even be more than one hundred and four, and frequently feel like a dinosaur...

But you're never
too big to hold.

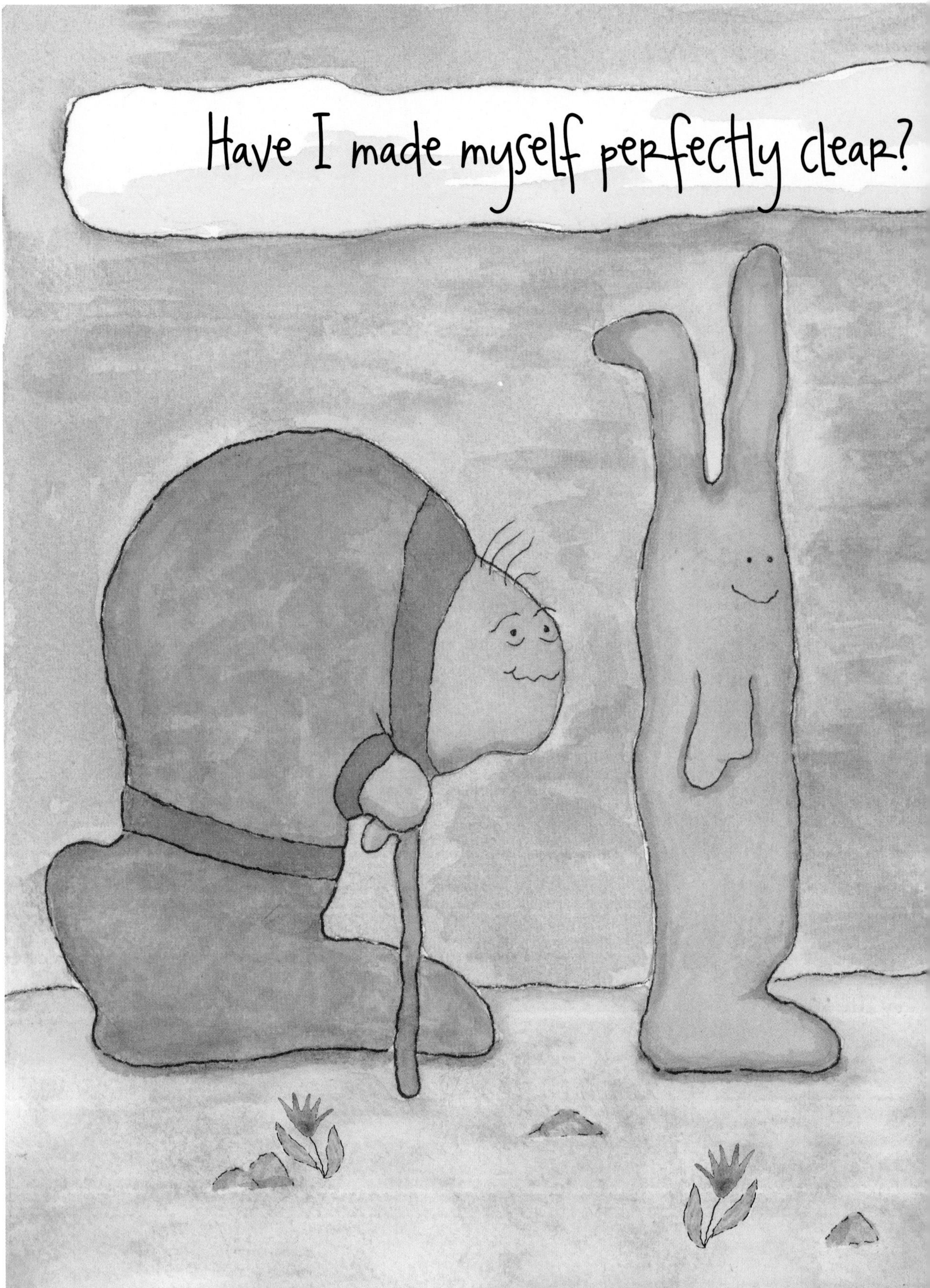
Have I made myself perfectly clear?

For I want you to listen, my dear:

No matter how old, or big, or strong...

You can be held
your whole
life long,

'Cause you're never, ever, never, EVER...

TOO BIG TO HOLD!

People Who Will Hold Me If I Ask

→ Piper

1. Mommy + Daddy
2. Grandma + Grampa
3. Oma + Opa
4. Auntie Chris + Uncle Tim
5. Uncle Patrick + ~~Uncle~~ Auntie Alex
6. Brady, Oskar, Claire, Samantha, Bjorn, Addie + Sophia
7. Godparents Christina + Brian
8. Natalie, Nicole + Baby Leo
9. Betsy + Mookie
10. Baby Teagan + MYSELF

It's more than a hug!

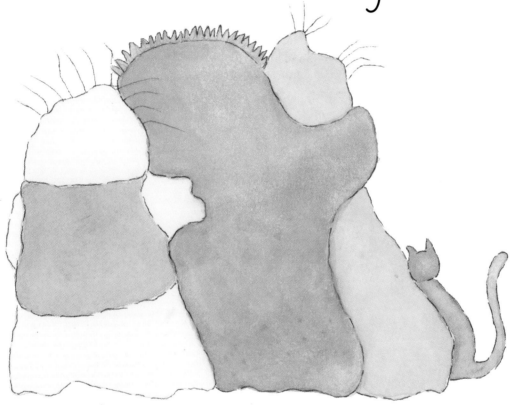

Please hold me for <u>one</u> <u>minute</u> or longer!

More To Read on Comforting Touch

For Kids

I Can Show You I Care: Compassionate Touch for Children
Sue Cotta and Gregory Crawford

You Hold Me and I'll Hold You
Jo Carson and Annie Cannon

Love You Forever
Robert Munch and Sheila McGraw

For Adults

From the Heart through the Hands and *Compassionate Touch*
Dawn Nelson

The Power of Touch
Phyllis K. Davis

Touching: The Human Significance of the Skin
Ashley Montagu

photo by Barbara Fabacher

BARBARA BASSETT learned about holding when she was 42, and very sick and scared in the hospital. Being held calmed her and helped her heal—and continues to do so, almost 20 years later.

She believes that if all of us were held at the right times (and let go of at the right times), we wouldn't need so much medicine, media, and "stuff."